JAPAN HOME

Inspirational Design Ideas

LISA PARRAMORE and CHADINE FLOOD GONG
Photography by NOBORU MURATA

TUTTLE PUBLISHING
Tokyo • Rutland, Vermont • Singapore

Published by Tuttle Publishing, an imprint of Periplus
Editions (HK) Ltd., with editorial offices at 364 Innovation
Drive, North Clarendon, Vermont 05759, USA, and 61 Tai
Seng Avenue, #02-12, Singapore 534167

Text copyright © 2009 Periplus Editions (HK) Ltd
Photographs © 2009 Noboru Murata
Photography coordinator: Kaoru Murata

ISBN 978-4-8053-1000-7

Distributed by:

North America, Latin America & Europe
Tuttle Publishing
364 Innovation Drive
North Clarendon, VT 05759-9436, U.S.A.
Tel: 1 (802) 773-8930; Fax: 1 (802) 773-6993
info@tuttlepublishing.com
www.tuttlepublishing.com

Japan
Tuttle Publishing
Yaekari Building, 3rd Floor
5-4-12 Osaki; Shinagawa-ku
Tokyo 141 0032
Tel: (81) 03 5437-0171; Fax: (81) 03 5437-0755
tuttle-sales@gol.com

Asia Pacific
Berkeley Books Pte Ltd
61 Tai Seng Avenue, #02-12
Singapore 534167
Tel: (65) 6280-1330; Fax: (65) 6280-6290
inquiries@periplus.com.sg
www.periplus.com

12 11 10 09   10 9 8 7 6 5 4 3 2 1

Printed in Singapore

TUTTLE PUBLISHING® is a registered trademark of Tuttle
Publishing, a division of Periplus Editions (HK) Ltd.

CONTENTS

DESIGNING
A JAPANESE
DREAM HOME

It is raining. If you are inside a typical Western home, you might not even be aware of the rain.

In a traditional Japanese home, the window openings are wide and the sills, if there are any, are low. The solid roof above spreads its eaves protectively around the house and frames the garden for you to enjoy during the rain. Seeing the garden glisten in the rain, you feel peace and serenity. The rain, the garden, the outside—they are all a part of your living space. Indeed, the Japanese word for home, *katei*, is a combination of the characters for house (*ka*) and garden (*tei*), reminding us that the ideal living space in Japan includes both.

As designers, we are accustomed to clients asking us to create spaces that are tranquil yet dramatic, understated yet elegant, and we enjoy guiding their journey towards a deeper understanding of Japanese aesthetics. Indeed, the serene atmosphere of the Japanese home is what attracts many Westerners, and the rooms and gardens shown on these pages convey that mood. This book will help you understand the form and function of Japanese spaces and the aesthetic intent behind them so that you may better pursue your dream.

Whether you plan to build a dream home from scratch or create a single special room, it requires an appreciation for the uniquely Japanese approach to beauty. While many concepts exist to describe and interpret beauty from a Japanese perspective, we mention two terms here that will serve well as an introduction.

The first is *sukiya*, an architectural style dating back to the sixteenth century when the practice of the tea ceremony solidified into the

Wood and bamboo figure prominently in a Japanese room. The soothing colors of nature create a subdued and tranquil atmosphere. A Japanese room, with its reliance on vertical and horizontal lines arranged in asymmetrical fashion, is the picture of simplicity.

Light is managed with elegance in Japanese homes. Paper *shoji* screens diffuse harsh sunlight to softly bathe a room in natural light, while the gold-leaf folding screen at the rear reflects light.

ritualized custom it is today. The Katsura Detached Palace in Kyoto, characterized by elegant proportions and restrained ornamentation, is considered the classic example of this type of building. Rejecting opulence and extravagance, the indigenous style of *sukiya* influenced residential architecture as well.

While *sukiya* refers to an architectural style, *shibui* refers to beauty itself, specifically, the highest level of beauty one can realize. An object worthy of being called *shibui* implies a quiet luxury, something simple and useful yet elegant. Fifty years have passed since readers of the American magazine *House Beautiful* were introduced at length to the concept. "*Shibui* describes a profound, unassuming, quiet feeling," wrote Elizabeth Gordon in the 1960 article. An object described as *shibui* "must have elements that make you want to examine it, study it, to look again and again. It must not reveal itself all at once." A lacquered doorknob might depict part of a flower; a screen painting might show a section of a tree trunk: it is up to the viewer to use his imagination to complete the scene. The homes and interiors in this book reflect the influence of *sukiya*-style architecture and are decorated with objects that may be called *shibui*.

This book will introduce you first to the Japanese house, room by room, in Chapter One, "Spaces in a Japanese House." Understanding the traditional blueprint will help you think about the aspects of the Japanese lifestyle that you might wish to adapt, such as removing shoes and storing them in a cabinet in the foyer, sleeping on a *futon* close to the mild aroma of *tatami* mats of woven straw, or relaxing in a deep soaking tub up to your shoulders with a view of a garden at the end of a busy day. It will also help you think about floor plans differently. You might opt to omit one or more permanent walls in favor of sliding partitions or expand the view of the garden through larger windows or openings.

If you have only a single room to work with, consider the interiors shown in the second chapter, "Tatami and Tea." Following the lead of the contemporary Japanese family whose post-war lifestyle resembles in many ways its Western counterpart, a single room may be all that is needed (or practical) to employ Japanese aesthetics. This room can function as a retreat from the hustle and bustle of the rest of the household, or a place to create an inviting experience for guests, whether for afternoon tea or an overnight stay.

Chapter Three discusses the use of accents and furnishings and how to make them work in any room, and the final chapter is devoted to the garden, the space that truly completes a Japanese home. Inherent in the Japanese philosophy of life is a keen sensitivity to nature and its rhythms, and the use of natural materials in our homes is part of what makes us feel connected to nature. The materials that

An essential consideration in planning a garden is how it looks from the interior. The garden, framed by the lines of the architecture, thus becomes a work of art.

Humble, natural materials such as wood and bamboo give the Japanese home a simple yet elegant feel.

comprise traditional *katei*—straw, paper, wood, bamboo, stone and water—are not disguised but rather treated to bring out their essence. Wood is left unpainted to better appreciate its grain and patina; paper is engineered for translucence and luminescence; rainwater is allowed to flow down a rain chain of shapely copper cups rather than hidden in a downspout. Yet, there are cases when a substitute material may be practical in a Western home without sacrificing the intended effect: a deep soaking tub made of fiberglass requires less maintenance than a traditional wooden *ofuro*; synthetic inserts for *shoji* panels still modulate light, minimizing concern over damage to the traditional *washi* paper. We hope the traditional examples provided in this book will inspire you to become more aesthetically perceptive, and where appropriate we will point out what options and adaptations a Westerner might wish to consider.

The skillful arrangement of materials and the architecture itself in asymmetrical fashion is equally important. One of the first writers to point this out to Westerners was Edward Morse in his 1886 publication, *Japanese Homes and Their Surroundings*, an indispensable volume that recorded the details of ordinary dwellings of the period. He noted with frustration the "intolerable monotony" of bilateral symmetry in American homes of the time in which "each half of the [fireplace]

mantel shall receive its half of a clock," and described for his Western audience how the Japanese aesthetic, more in keeping with natural patterns, can be deeply satisfying. Strive in your décor for the more dynamic and sophisticated approach of asymmetrical balance.

Just as important as the use of natural materials is an absence of clutter. If we are in tune with Japanese aesthetics, an awareness of how art interacts with space informs the way we go about decorating our homes. A pleasing tension results in the art of Japanese flower arranging, when branches, leaves and finally blossoms are brought together in an energetic silhouette. A single painted folding screen with a scene that meanders across six panels has more impact than a series of discrete framed paintings.

While on this journey, some might ask the question: Is the Japanese home a way of building or is it a way of living? The premise we find most helpful to begin with is that the Japanese home is a way of *feeling*. What is it about the Japanese home that evokes the feelings of peace and serenity? How can you connect with nature's rhythms and seasons in your approach to décor? We will help you understand why the Japanese home induces a particular mood so you can better articulate it in the pursuit of your own home's design. After all, isn't that what dreaming is all about?

FLEXIBLE SPACES
IN A JAPANESE HOME

The traditional Japanese house shows a great roof to the world and accommodates a number of flexible spaces within. To grasp the essence of how the Japanese house is organized, observe in this chapter how the space contained in a room changes according to use. Sliding partitions not only conserve space, they also allow adjacent rooms to become a larger room when needed. Movable walls are also useful to incorporate the garden into the living space.

To give your home a Japanese feel, consider ways to open up the room, even if your space is small. Exposing the rafters and trusses in a room expands the volume of the room and offers us a connection to the architecture that is absent in our familiar world of plastered ceilings. Acquaint yourself with the natural grain of various woods and trim out the ceiling with bands of wood to better define the plain walls.

Look for opportunities to bring the outside in. Open up a wall to the back yard and install a large expanse of glass. Use one or more sets of sliding glass doors, fixed glazing, or a combination that suits you. These days, a number of architects and designers are turning to accordion-style glass doors that fold out of the way, expanding the living space to encompass the garden.

A large expanse of glass warrants an equally thoughtful window treatment. A bank of *shoji* panels along the interior of the glass serves multiple functions: it pleasantly diffuses sunlight, offers a surface upon which trees and foliage cast ever-changing shadows, provides privacy when needed and a bright white reflective surface to cover the dark glass at night.

The design concepts above are best executed with a heavy dose of restraint. Japanese aesthetics is much more than simple minimalism or "less is more"; it is highly developed through centuries and is skillfully underplayed. To borrow an analogy from music, the late Dizzie Gillespie once remarked, "The notes that are not played are as important as the notes that *are* played" to describe the appeal of jazz. Similarly, the role of empty space in a Japanese room is just as important as what is tangible.

Movable walls, which modulate both the size and amount of natural light in a room, take several forms, including translucent *shoji* panels and lattice wooden partitions.

LEAVING THE OUTSIDE WORLD BEHIND

In the Japanese house, transitions are deliberate: from the public sphere to the private and from the exterior to the interior. Create a sense of discovery with a handsome gate flanked by a wall, fence or hedge. A bridge that crosses water suggests that the outside world is to be left behind. Alternatively, crossing a dry stream of pebbles or cobbles offers the suggestion of water. What lies beyond is for you and your guests, not for passersby.

At the entrance to the house is another intentional transition, a small tiled or concrete vestibule called the *genkan*. This is a ground-level space where shoes are removed before stepping up to the interior proper to avoid tracking in dirt.

As shoeless interiors become more popular outside Asia, the organization and décor of the *genkan* are of great interest. A large slab or stone at the threshold with a step up signifies the expectation that shoes shall be removed here. Visit your local stone yard and personally select a thick, sturdy rock to be used as a shoe removal stone, or *kutsunugi-ishi*, the width of which should be in proportion to the door.

If your house does not have a step up, you can achieve a similar look just outside the front door by replacing an ordinary welcome mat with a beautiful flat stone slab surrounded by pebbles. Search antiques galleries for a *geta-bako*, a cabinet for shoe storage and sometimes umbrellas. If older cabinets are not large enough for Western shoes, a custom-made cabinet may be in order. Walking about the house in slippers or stockinged feet is an overlooked ingredient in creating a quiet, serene atmosphere.

野々市町指定有形文化財

Opposite The ceramic-tiled gate, or *mon*, in the shape of a warrior's helmet, reveals the status of the family that has lived on this land in northern Japan for eleven generations. The fence, or *itabei*, was built with scorched wooden planks to resist rot in snow country.
Above The gate at this estate frames a view of a moss-covered tree trunk, anticipating the verdant garden beyond.
Below In contrast to the gate, irregular stepping stones convey a rustic feeling.

Left Stone paving on either side of the threshold unites the house and garden. In the rear, a small cupboard is useful for storing slippers.

Above and right The commanding roof on this mountain home north of Kyoto signifies a cozy and protected abode within. Oil paper umbrellas, called *bangasa*, offer shelter from the elements. The word *ban* refers to things that are coarse, simple or humble, and serves to distinguish them from the more elegant paper *wagasa* umbrellas.

Left Intricate latticework creates playful shadows throughout the day while allowing air to circulate in humid Kyoto.

Above Shoes are removed in this *genkan*, paved with earthenware tiles, before ascending to the interior proper.

Left The paving stones in this courtyard garden form an indirect path to the front door. Such a path is considered more interesting and makes a short walk feel longer.

Right A lattice door partially screens a courtyard entry, adding a sense of discovery to the journey from the outside world to the private home. The rhythm of this cut stone path next to a rock garden illustrates the Japanese design concept of asymmetrical balance.

Left A screen mounted in a wooden stand, known as a *tsuitate*, is often placed at the entrance as a partition to separate the entryway from the living space beyond. Such freestanding screens may be painted or feature latticework.

Below The wide step in this *genkan* has a built-in sliding storage compartment suitable for storing shoes. The owner of this Sukiya-style home placed this unusual art object in the *tatami* room to symbolically separate the secular outside world from the sacred space within.

Above A storage cupboard was added to the entryway of this 200-year-old home in Tokyo. The resulting niche is perfect for the owner's thoughtful display of a scroll and seasonal flower arrangement.

Above right An earthen floor contrasts with a wood and stucco storage cabinet in the entryway of this 100-year-old farmhouse, or *minka*. This look can be achieved in concrete with today's increasingly sophisticated staining techniques.

Right Placing shoes facing outward so that they are easy to slip on is expected etiquette in Japan, where outdoor shoes are not worn inside. Wooden sandals called *geta* slip on easily for a seamless transition to the garden.

THE JAPANESE **LIVING ROOM**

The photographs on these pages reveal the elegant simplicity of Japanese rooms and their subdued colors, whether or not they have Western-style furniture. A traditional Japanese living room does not have many pieces of furniture and is designed for sitting on *tatami* mats on the floor, preferably with a view out to the garden.

The concept of movable walls offers practical solutions to challenges some might face when deciding how to make the most efficient use of space. Fiona O'Neill, an architect in Sea Ranch, California, used this approach in her home to eliminate the need for a separate guest bedroom. By installing sliding *shoji* screens in the main living room, she is able to close off part of the space for guests when needed. Another space saving technique we have observed in a home commissioned by artist Nancy Ziegler Nodelman involves the use of sliding partitions to hide or reveal recesses for a home office, kitchen pantry and laundry—even a trundle bed!

Left A room surrounded by gardens is the epitome of the Japanese living space. Minimal furniture contributes to a feeling of spaciousness and tranquility.

Right Horizontal and vertical lines create order and harmony in a Japanese room. Artistic expression can be found in the choice of scroll and flower arrangement in the recessed alcove as well as the painted scene on the doors of the low cupboard.

Left In summer, room-dividing partitions are sometimes replaced with *sudare*, woven blinds of reed or bamboo. Such devices facilitate air circulation and render objects behind in gauzy silhouette. The decorative tassels have hooks that allow the blinds to be rolled up when desired.
Above Wood trusses attached to vertical posts support an intricate vaulted ceiling and line up perfectly with the sliding *shoji* partitions.

Left A low table is set for tea in a *tatami* floor room with a view of the garden. The raised platform in the rear offers a place to display fresh flowers.
Below Blackened pine timbers wrapped in rice-straw rope provide a striking contrast to the Western-style furniture in the sitting alcove of this eighteenth-century farmhouse.

Right *Shoji* screens not only filter light and provide privacy, they can also be adjusted to frame the scenery outside, such as this bamboo grove. Bamboo, the fastest growing woody species on earth, can grow up to 60 centimeters per day until reaching maturity in a matter of weeks, earning its reputation as a renewable resource.
Opposite Movable partitions known as *fusuma* are covered with gold-leaf paper, reflecting light in interior rooms. They allow the size of a room to be changed according to need.

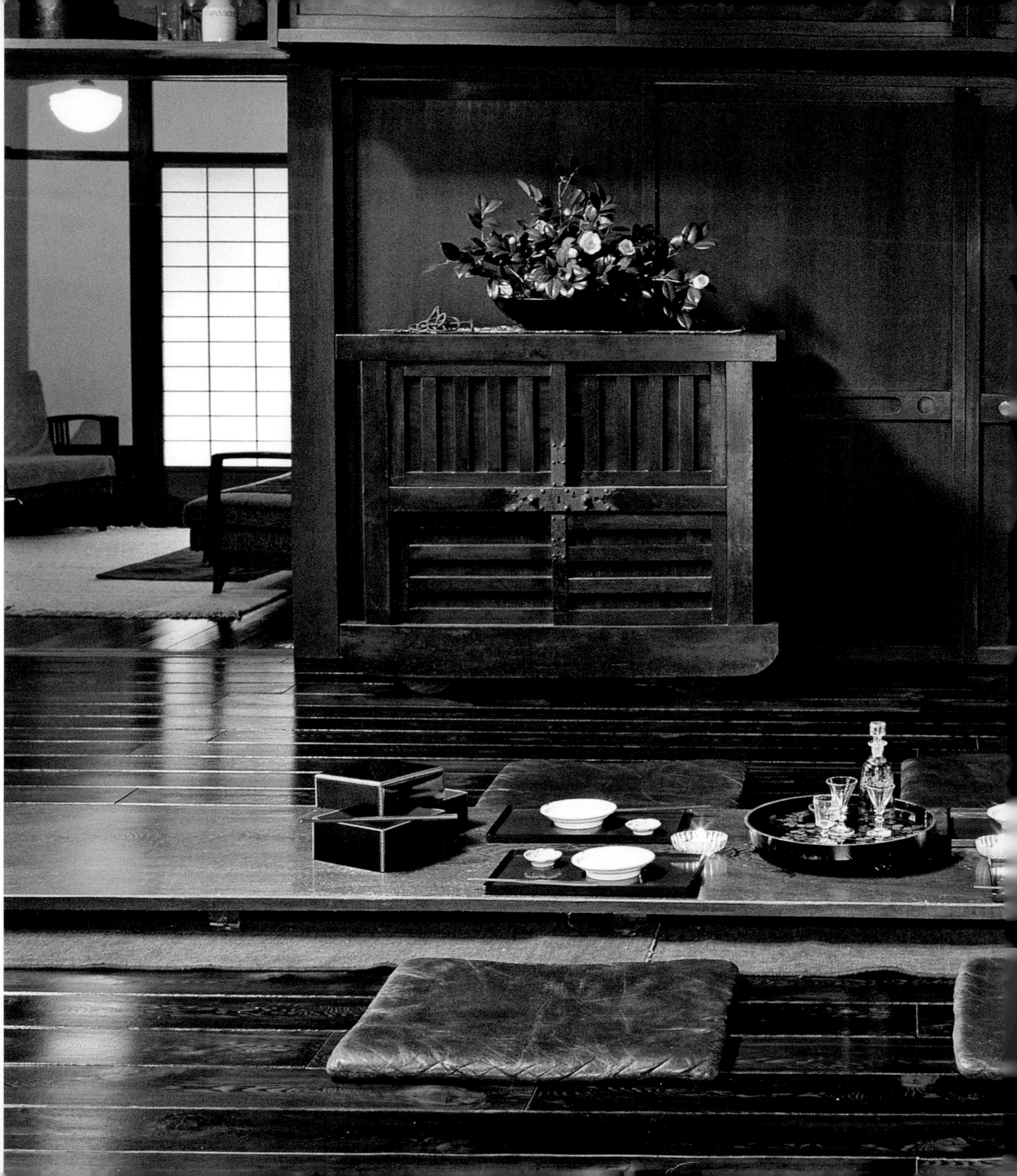

A PLACE FOR
DINING

Like living rooms, spaces for dining can be in either a permanent dining room with a Western-style table and chairs or a *tatami* mat room with a low table where you are seated on comfortable cushions. Keep decorations on the table to a minimum—perhaps a stone trivet or an iron tea kettle. The cuisine and the dinnerware on which it is served are the main attractions. Notice the beauty of the ceramics and lacquerware on these tables that elevate everyday items to works of art.

A cozy way to dine is to use a low table, called a *kotatsu*, with an electric heating element fastened to its undersurface. Sometimes, the *kotatsu* has a sunken floor beneath for one's feet. Many families in Japan dine at such tables with their stockinged feet tucked under a thick quilt sandwiched between the removable table top and frame. Like the fireplace in a Western home, the *kotatsu* is a central gathering place for meals, playing cards, watching television or simply sitting around and chatting.

Hardwood floors with multiple layers of lacquer contrast with the low wooden table. The square cushions for sitting are known as *zabuton*.

Right and below right These two photos illustrate two types of *kotatsu*, the low table used for dining. The sunken area in the photo on the right allows for comfortable seating while dining. During cold weather, a quilt can be placed between the table's frame and its removable top, creating a cozy place to keep one's legs warm. The window opening is intentionally low to frame a view visible from a seated position. The table in the photo at bottom right is portable, and one usually sits on square cushions known as *zabuton*.

Opposite A simple garden makes a pleasant backdrop for this outdoor dining space. The garden is a testament to clever composition: a foreground of gravel backed by a low hedge and tall bamboo in the rear add depth to a narrow space.

Top and above The subdued appearance of lacquerware belies the laborious process used to create it. With a luster of seemingly endless depth, handcrafted lacquerware makes an essential aesthetic contribution to an authentic Japanese meal.

Above The artistic display of dishes is as aesthetically
important as the meal itself. A glass top covers
this antique dining table lacquered with gold leaf.

Right Cooking at the table is a treasured social experience. The oversized hood extracts smoke and cooking smells when cooking is done on the three built-in gas rings, concealed by panels matching the oak table.

Below A dining room with Western-style furniture can be enhanced by the use of a six-paneled screen painting. When decorating your own dining room, select a screen painting that complements the proportions of the dining room table.

THE VERANDA

Long before the term "outside room" became popular in the West to describe patios equipped with an array of amenities, the Japanese took advantage of the space beneath the wide roof overhang of their homes to create a special type of veranda. Known as *engawa* in Japanese, it is a porch area beneath the eaves that functions as an interface between the house and garden. The traditional *engawa* is made of wood or bamboo and may be part of the inside or the outside depending upon the season. In severe weather, wooden shutters may enclose the *engawa*, rendering it a corridor of sorts. During the summer, the wooden shutters can be removed, transforming the *engawa* into a shady deck.

As wooden shutters have become less common, the *engawa* has also come to refer to a narrow exterior deck that runs parallel with one or more sides of the house. This is a simple addition that can be made to almost any home. Extend the eaves at least a meter (three feet or more) from the house so that they cover the space completely. Wide overhangs also act as the visual upper frame of the scenery outside.

Translucent panels of *shoji* may line the interior side of the *engawa* while heavier doors made of wood or glass slide along the exterior side. Both sets of sliding panels can be pushed aside during warm weather, allowing you to sit inside but feel as though you are outside.

Position *shoji* panels on the inside of the glass walls or doors on tracks that allow you to slide and stack them against a solid wall to maximize the opening to the outside or to close it off at night for privacy. Stacking the *shoji* panels beyond the opening gives the pleasing illusion that the glass walls or doors are wider than they actually are. If the location of the structural posts in your home prevents a wide opening, create the impression of one by installing a pair of glass walls or sliding glass doors on either side of the post and a *shoji* panel to hide the wall in between.

Posts frame a dry landscape garden next to a wooden veranda. Note the shoe stone in place of a wooden step.

Above An *engawa* without railings helps integrate the garden with the house. **Below** *Shoji* panels slide back to reveal sliding glass doors and a view of the garden at this Kyoto home. The veranda allows one to enjoy the garden from the shade of the eaves.

Right Lacquer on this wooden veranda in Akita, a part of Japan that receives heavy snowfall, shields it from the elements. The transom along the edge of the overhang further protects it. The way the posts and transom frame the garden is reminiscent of Japanese folding screen paintings.

Above The wooden *engawa* acts as an intermediate space between the house and garden. Sliding *shoji* panels enclose and protect the interior *tatami* rooms.

Left This veranda, made of bamboo poles, frames the view of a large water basin arrangement.

Right Wood planks interspersed with narrow bamboo poles makes an interesting contrast to the broader bamboo poles on the veranda of this tea hut.

Below A veranda that wraps around a house with multiple entrances to the rooms allows one to interact with the garden while moving from one part of the house to another.

AN ELEGANT **SLEEPING AREA**

There is nothing quite like visiting a traditional Japanese inn in the mountains and being welcomed to your small room with a fresh cup of green tea. After visiting the local sights, which may, in fact, consist of nothing more strenuous than bathing in the resort's natural hot springs, you return to your room to find a fresh *futon* rolled out for you directly on the *tatami* mat floor. The fragrance of the straw mats and the crisp mountain air, not to mention the *saké* you sipped at dinner, may well induce the best sleep you have had in a long time.

If you are inclined to re-create such bliss in your own home, remember that *futon* must be stored away during the day to allow the *tatami* flooring to breathe and they should be aired in the sun regularly. This application is of particular interest to people who host overnight guests but lack a spare bedroom. It is also obviously a space-saving solution when the room can be used for other activities during the day.

If a Japanese room has a bed, it is likely to be a platform bed that is low to the floor. Available in the West are platform beds made with *tatami* which may offer the best of both worlds for those unable to cover an entire room with the straw mats. Soft lighting made from translucent paper sets the mood for a restful night's sleep.

Left A *futon* on *tatami* flooring is a surprisingly comfortable way to sleep.

Above A light cotton *yukata* robe has been placed on the *futon* for the guest's use. The lovely *shoji* screens in this room have a pattern of squares, in contrast to the usual rectangles. The folding screen, or *byobu*, makes an elegant piece of art. Before the advent of indoor heating, it was a device used to protect the sleeper from cold drafts.

Left and below Surrounded by the elegance of a *sukiya*-style room, one is assured of a restful night's sleep. In summertime, woven reed blinds allow the room to ventilate.

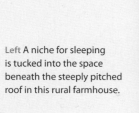

Left A niche for sleeping is tucked into the space beneath the steeply pitched roof in this rural farmhouse.

Left and below At a *ryokan*, or Japanese inn, a *yukata* cotton robe and waist tie have been folded and placed in a tray for the overnight guest. The lacquered floor lamp, or *andon*, bathes the room in a soft glow.

Left and below Contemporary bedrooms feature platform beds that are low to the floor.

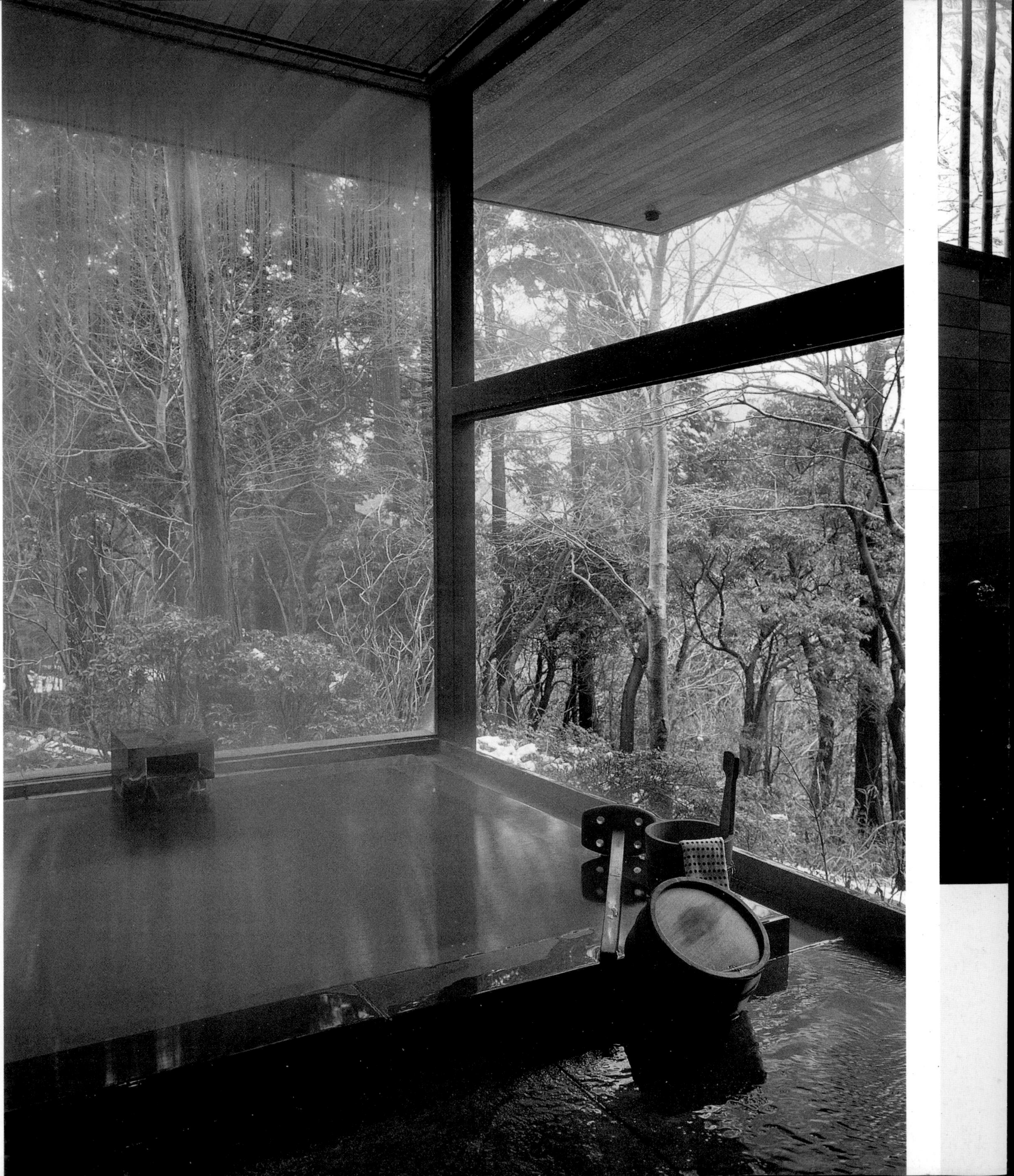

THE JAPANESE **BATH**

A volcanically active country, Japan has thousands of natural hot springs, or *onsen*, scattered along its length and breadth where its people have long sought relaxation and healing. The therapeutic aspects of hot springs influenced the design of residential bathrooms after indoor plumbing became the norm.

There is a distinct area in the bathroom for changing clothes, with a sink for brushing teeth and washing hands, and another space for the toilet. Beyond the changing area is a separate space dedicated solely to bathing, emphasizing the indulgent aspect of the bath. It is here that one scrubs with soap and water before entering the bathtub, or *ofuro*.

A bathtub made of fragrant cypress, with a small garden visible while seated in the tub, elevates bathing to a soul-cleansing ritual. Other materials used today for tubs include tile, concrete and fiberglass. The main requirement is that the tub must be deep enough to soak up to the neck. A drain in the floor of the bathroom captures overflow from the tub.

The garden outside the bath need not be large to achieve the desired effect, but it must be private. A variety of fence panels made of bamboo, wood or reed can screen off the garden for privacy. If this is not possible, a *shoji* screen can be used to cover the window without blocking the light. Placing a potted plant with interesting foliage outside the screen can create beautiful shadows that enhance the atmosphere of your Japanese bath.

To give your bathroom further Japanese touches, mount a waist-high wooden *tansu* chest topped by a raised sink to create a unique vanity. A length of bamboo, outfitted with metal hardware and mounted horizontally on the wall, makes a fine towel rack. Bring nature into the bath by running tiles of river rock along the floor and up the walls. A *shoji* panel makes the perfect door to hide shelves of towels or, used as a sliding pocket door, to conceal the toilet. Place a small garden lantern next to the sink with a candle inside for atmosphere.

Above This contemporary bath is unified with the garden through clever use of materials. The reed blinds hanging outside the glass echo the wood paneling above the tub. Like the *ofuro* itself, the bucket and stool are made from rot-resistant Japanese cypress, and are used for washing onself prior to entering the tub.

Far left Window placement in a Japanese bathroom is important. The sill should be low enough to allow the person using the tub to enjoy the view.
Left and below left Accessories such as a wooden stool and bucket made of fragrant cypress can bring the smell of the forest to your bath when a wooden tub is impractical. The bucket may be used to rinse off or to scoop hot water from the tub to accustom your body to the hot temperature of the bath.

Right A wooden lid keeps water warm between uses, particularly important in tubs where the water is heated by an external stove. Another way to add fragrance to the bath is to float *yuzu*, a type of Japanese lime that sophisticated chefs are introducing to today's global cuisine.

TATAMI AND TEA

The tea ceremony occupies a unique place in Japanese culture. More than a social gathering for drinking tea, it is a sacred, almost religious ritual called *chanoyu*. Through focused concentration of the mind, *chanoyu* is, for host and guests alike, a purification of the inner self. Procedures and movements may appear mysterious and esoteric to the novice, but that is the point: the whole is a gracefully orchestrated experience that is greater than the sum of its parts.

Just as important as the ritual itself is the setting in which it occurs, hence the enormous and lasting influence of the tea ceremony on Japan's architecture, interiors and gardens. The buildings and rooms shown in this chapter illustrate what is known as *sukiya*-style architecture, which includes the tea room or tea house and accessory structures in the garden.

The tea room and associated décor strike a nostalgic note for the Japanese, and the typical single family home, though modern in every other respect, frequently has one Japanese room, or *washitsu*, where the *sukiya* tradition lives on. This is true whether or not anyone living in the home actually practices the tea ceremony.

The tea room or tea house is also evocative of what many Westerners find attractive about Japanese décor, so it serves as an excellent template for a special place in our own homes. Such an exceptional space might be a cozy parlor in which to serve a home-cooked meal to guests. Alternatively, a room once designed to facilitate rigorous concentration of the mind may be just what we might use today for quiet activities such as reading, yoga, meditation or simply an afternoon nap.

Opposite A large room covered with wall-to-wall *tatami* mats is suitable for entertaining guests. The juxtaposition of the low wooden tables with the rectangular, black cloth-bordered *tatami* mats creates dramatic aesthetic tension. The dark portable metal charcoal brazier is known as a *hibachi*, literally "fire bowl".

Left A low window covered with a *shoji* panel bathes this room in soft light. Covering the window during tea ceremony ensures concentration on the ritual.

CREATING A JAPANESE TEA ROOM

"If the heart is pure, the tea will taste good." This phrase epitomizes the philosophy behind the tea ceremony and serves as a gentle reminder that a tea room should be a simple space free of excess ornamentation. Humble materials such as wood, paper and straw, subdued colors, and the restrained display of art adorn the tea rooms on these pages.

The feel of a Japanese tea room begins with a *tatami*-covered floor—padded rice-straw mats left in their natural color. The number of *tatami* mats used, each approximately 90 by 180 centimeters (3 feet by 6 feet), determines the ultimate size of a room. If outfitting an entire room is not feasible, a *tatami*-covered platform may be a practical substitute.

For the walls, use sand paint in a restrained color such as ochre or moss, or go a step further and use plaster mixed with bits of straw for a lovely organic texture. Trim the ceiling with wood or perhaps grass cloth.

A recessed alcove, known as a *tokonoma*, is the crown jewel of the tea room. Lit discreetly from behind a false wall, it serves as a display space for a hanging scroll and seasonal flower arrangement or some other treasured piece of art. Finish the alcove with a wooden post and a raised platform, and add staggered shelves or built-in storage adjacent to the *tokonoma*.

Above and right These two examples illustrate the restrained approach to tea room décor. Wide boards with an interesting grain are used on the ceiling of the room on the right.

Right A portable box-shaped container, called a *hibachi*, lined with heatproof material and filled with charcoal, is used here to boil water for tea but is also traditionally used to heat homes. Square cushions called *zabuton* are comfortable to sit on and can be used as a color accent to offset the earthy tones of the tea room.

Below A wood-trimmed ceiling and mud-plastered walls add to the authenticity of this traditional tea room.

Below right The false wall in this *tokonoma* frames the alcove and conceals a light source that highlights the scroll and flower arrangement. The pole at the corner of the *tokonoma*, called a *tokobashira*, retains its original bark, adding a simple but elegant touch.

Above Notice in this room how a band of trim runs above the sliding *shoji* doors, alcove display spaces, and closet doors, giving the tall ceilings a more human scale.

Right A bold indigo-hued wall hanging replaces the usual scroll in this *tokonoma* display. The flower arrangement in front echoes the shape and colors of the woven design.

Above An antique two-panel folding screen, known as a tea screen, complements the straw-colored *tatami* in this tea room and makes a lovely backdrop for an antique iron tea pots and ceramic tea caddy.

Right Staggered shelves, or *chigai-dana*, are commonly placed adjacent to the recessed *tokonoma*, separated by a thin partition, and may also be used to display art objects. Cupboards with sliding doors are used for storage.

Above Cedar makes a striking post, or *tokobashira*, for this decorative alcove. The window at the right is unusual in its shape as well as the diagonal pattern of the bamboo lattice.

Far left In this tea room, a narrow flower vase has been affixed to the rustic *toko-bashira* post.

Left A preparation area adjacent to the tea room allows for the cleaning and storage of tea bowls and utensils. Known as a *mizuya*, the word literally means "water room."

Below Light filters gently through matchstick reed blinds, creating delicate shadows in this tea room. Coordinating the items displayed in the *tokonoma* alcove with the season or special occasion is part of the attention to detail for which *sukiya*-style interiors are known. In this *tokonoma*, Kyoto's summer Gion Festival is referenced with a small offering stand and arrangement of rice ears and *sakaki* leaves.

Above While a rustic tea room is typically four and a half mats in size, a formal tea room might have as many as twenty-four mats and be large enough to entertain a substantial number of guests. The use of reflective gold-leaf paper to cover the built-in storage cabinets creates a sense of formality.

Right An intricate lattice window filters a view of the garden. The use of natural materials, such as the wood lattice and the *shoji* panels, defines the elegant simplicity of tea room architecture and décor.

TATAMI AND TEA

THE JAPANESE TEA HOUSE

Like the tea room, the tea house is inspired by the same restrained design of refined rusticity. Whether a simple hut with a mere four and a half mats or a larger dwelling with rooms for various sized gatherings, the tea house is usually nestled within a tea garden that provides a serene natural setting to prepare one for participation in a tea ceremony. Although it has become common to use the term tea house loosely when thinking of a Japanese garden building, the photographs here will introduce you to the range of structures associated with the tea house, one of which might be suitable as a model for your back yard.

The importance of transitions discussed in the first chapter returns here to play a role in the layout of the tea garden. The journey towards the tea house should be experiential, an opportunity to set aside the demands of the day and anticipate a rewarding interlude. To achieve this, the grounds surrounding the tea house are divided with a gate between an outer garden and an inner garden, with a path of stepping stones laid out in circuitous fashion. Misting the stepping stone path before a guest arrives refreshes its appearance, hence the term *roji*, which literally means "dewy path." Places to pause along the *roji* are thoughtfully positioned: a stone lantern stands next to the path where light might be needed; a stone basin allows guests to rinse their hands and mouth, and a bench in a simple enclosure outside the tea house permits a rest while waiting to be summoned by the host with a gentle gong. While lingering in the tea garden, the mind is readied for the ritual inside.

Above A waiting bench, or *machi-ai*, offers a comfortable spot for tea ceremony guests to view the garden before being summoned by their host. The structure echoes the rustic simplicity of the tea house itself.
Left A framed opening marks the transition from the busy outside world to the quiet space within the tea house.
Opposite A rustic stone path surrounded by gravel and understated plantings sets a contemplative mood for a tea ceremony. The garden is swept clean and watered to give it a fresh appearance for guests approaching the tea house.

Left *Wabi-sabi*, an aesthetic concept that implies tasteful restraint and rustic simplicity, is evident at the entrance to the Kankyuan tea room at the Mushakoji Senke tea school in Kyoto. The pine needles have been swept carefully about the stepping stone path.

Above A shapely stone serves as a basin for rinsing hands and mouth, bringing an element of water to the tea garden.

Above The journey from the outside world to the intimate setting of the tea house begins in the outer garden. The gate and bamboo fence indicate the transition along the *roji* to the inner garden, where the guest is one step closer to leaving the outside world behind. The term *roji*, which means "dewy path," implies both the physical and mental journey along the stone walkway towards the seclusion of the tea room.

Above The choice of materials is humble, as evidenced by the packed earth floor, or *doma*, at the entrance porch to this tea house.

Right Wood, paper and stone: the elegant use of humble materials characterizes *sukiya*-style architecture.

Above A waiting bench, or *machi-ai*, has been positioned close to an old tree. The Japanese revere the beauty that comes from the patina of age, expressed in this mature, moss-covered tree trunk.

TATAMI AND TEA

Left A simpler structure than the tea house, the *azumaya* is an open-air pavilion that offers a restful setting from which to view the garden.

Below A garden is an integral part of a tea house and should give the impression of being effortlessly connected to it, as shown here. The scroll hanging in the *tokonoma* illustrates the beauty of Japanese calligraphy, or *shodo*.

Opposite Access to this tea house is through a low "crawl door," or *nijiriguchi*, originally designed to prevent samurai from entering with their swords. It obliges the tea ceremony guest to stoop before entering the tea house, a gentle reminder that the event about to take place necessitates a humble and reverent state of mind. The opening itself frames a scene of a meandering stepping stone path that invites the viewer to mentally complete the scene.

THE HEARTH

A fireplace is nearly ubiquitous in a Western living room, providing both warmth and a major design element. Its counterpart in a traditional Japanese room is the *irori*, or sunken hearth, with a pot hook suspended above. It, too, can be a beautiful focal point in a Japanese-inspired room.

The sunken hearth is usually a square pit in the middle of the room. If the hearth is in a *tatami* room, a removable *tatami* cover is placed on top, flush with the rest of the floor, when the *irori* is not in use. The pot hook, or *jizaikagi*, supports an iron kettle for boiling water for tea and has a lever allowing it to be raised or lowered. The lever of the pot hook can be a decorative element itself, featuring the shape of a fish or other motif related to cooking.

If an open hearth is not feasible, you can still transform the kettle and hook combination into an attractive design element compatible with your fireplace. Iron kettles with subtly textured designs are widely available, and traditional pot or kettle hooks can be found at galleries specializing in Japanese antiques. Suspend the hook and kettle combination from the ceiling so that it hovers over a wide hearth or over a *tatami* mat platform where the straw color of the *tatami* will beautifully set off the black kettle.

Above In a traditional farmhouse near Kyoto, charcoal glows in an open hearth while a bamboo tray holds a tea set.
Opposite The image of an iron kettle suspended from a hook over a fire pit pleasantly takes one back to the days when we relied upon fire for cooking and warmth.

Above In snowy northern Japan, a 200-year-old *minka* farmhouse has a simple *irori* built into the hardwood floor. **Left** A small square pit is all that is needed for boiling tea in this *tatami* room. Accessories to the *irori* include a feather brush for dusting away the ashes.

Left An antique silk folding tea screen provides an exquisite backdrop for a portable charcoal brazier, or *hibachi*.
Below A sixteenth-century iron kettle inscribed with Japanese *kanji* characters is suspended from a pot hook, or *jizaikagi*. A hook and kettle combination makes an intriguing conversation piece displayed next to a modern fireplace with a wide hearth.

Above This *kutsu-chawan*, or shoe bowl, owes its name to its unusual shape. The subdued colors and thick glaze of the tea bowl are characteristic of Oribe pottery, named after the distinguished tea master of sixteenth-century Japan. A sweet is often served first, to help reduce the bitter taste of the *matcha*, a variety of finely powdered green tea that is whisked to a frothy brew.

Right Guests at a tea ceremony may be offered tobacco, smoked through a slender pipe.

Opposite A wooden container designed to hold burning charcoal, called a *hibachi*, is used here as a display space for a tea set.

TEA IMPLEMENTS

For the tea ceremony practitioner, great care is taken when it comes to selecting the right containers to store tea, the utensils used to prepare it, and the bowls or *chawan* in which to serve it. A small, elegant tea caddy of lacquer belies the labor of love taken to craft it. Impossibly thin tea scoops and delicate whisks made of bamboo are testament to the careful ritual the tea host observes to make tea. Collectively known as *chadogu*, authentic tea implements add beauty to a room with a Japanese flavor. Inspecting and admiring *chadogu* is part of the etiquette by which the tea ceremony guest shows gratitude towards the host.

The *chawan* or tea bowl is the centerpiece of the tea ceremony. Handleless tea bowls are a credit to Japan's continued excellence in pottery. Greatly admired are those that are of imperfect shape or beauty, such as the one shown on the left. There is a saying in Japanese that describes this special aesthetic of imperfection: *musakui no sakui* or "the intention of no intention."

Above, right top and bottom Cleanliness is an important aspect of the tea ceremony, developed before modern plumbing became commonplace. Above, a wooden container specifically for the disposal of waste water sits next to a tray of common tea implements. In the photo above right, a box of attractively arranged charcoal is accompanied by a white feather attached to a wooden handle for dusting ashes away. The cloth hanging from the post in the photo at right is used for drying hands.

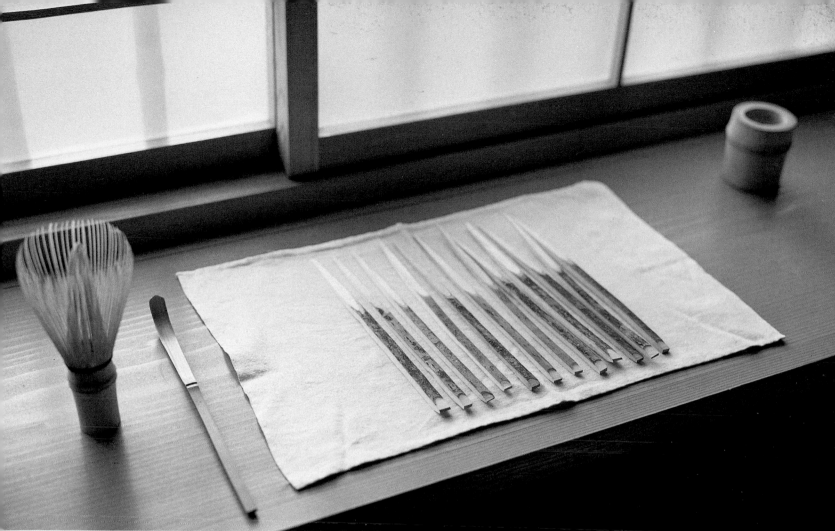

Above Delicately proportioned tea scoops are used to pick up just the right amount of the green powder used to make *matcha*, the frothy whisked brew used in the tea ceremony.

Right and far right Maples leaves (right) and bamboo leaves (far right) adorn these lacquered tea caddies. Motifs from nature underpin many Japanese artistic endeavors.

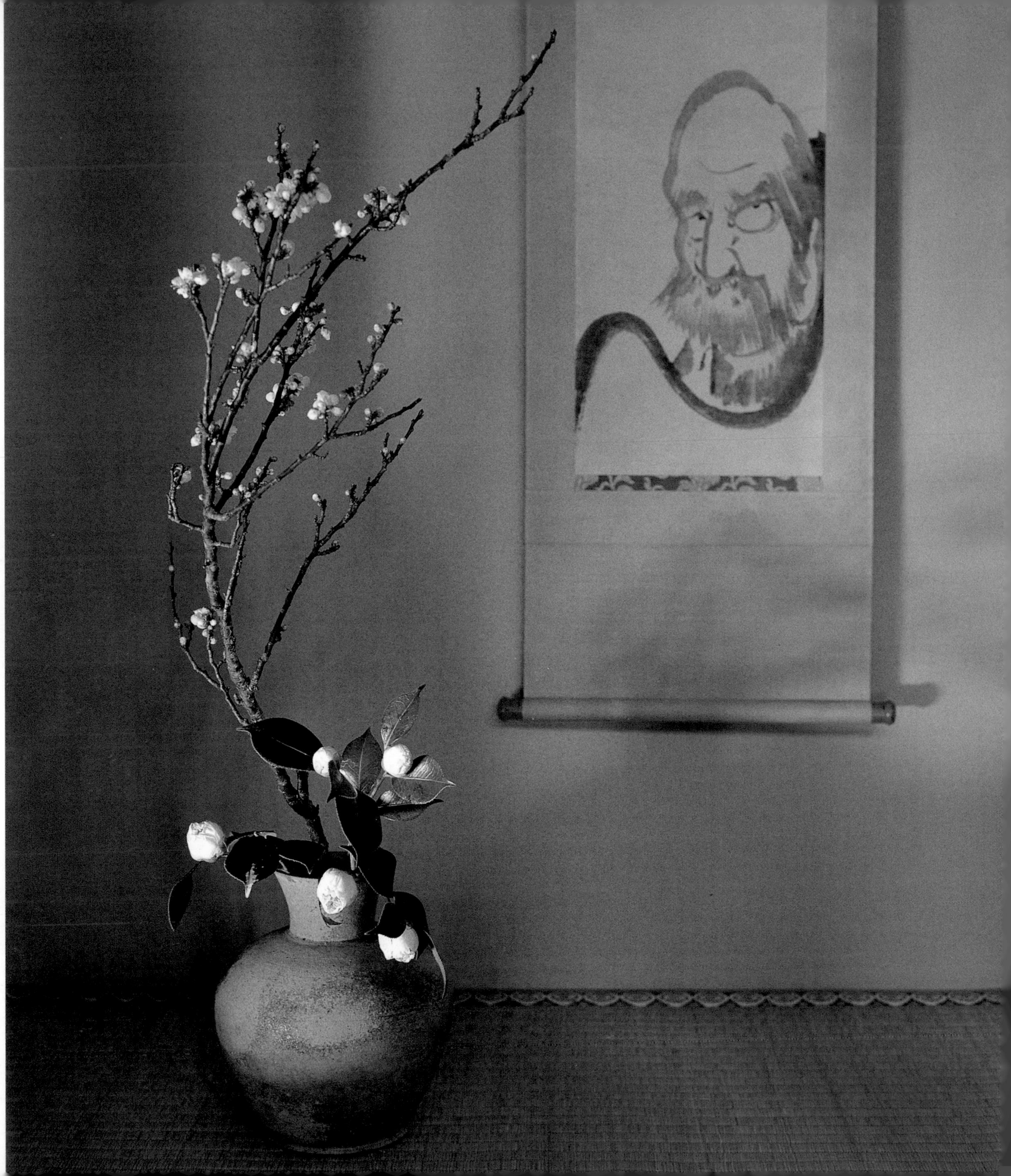

Left An arrangement of camellias and plum blossoms suggests movement and seems to echo the lines of the scroll.

Right The dark green *tokonoma* alcove sets off a vase of white lilies. This is an example of how the surrounding space was taken into consideration, making the backdrop, in effect, a part of the composition.

THE ART OF IKEBANA

The display space of the *tokonoma* is a special place to view a treasured thing, making it a favored setting for a Japanese flower arrangement, or *ikebana*. Unlike a Western vase of flowers viewed from 360 degrees, an *ikebana* composition is intended to be viewed face on. A skillful arrangement depends not only on the use of blossoms but also the foliage and branches, and great attention is paid to shape, line and form. Even the space where the arrangement is to be displayed and how the sun shines into the interior are taken into consideration.

Virtually anything that holds water can be used as a container, from ceramic vases to bamboo baskets to blocks of stone, and the shape of the vessel dictates the way the flowers are arranged. According to the Ikenobo School, the oldest school of *ikebana*, one must pay attention to how the plant material grows in nature and should try to express its unique character in the arrangement. For example, if a branch grows sideways in nature, it should be used in this fashion in *ikebana*.

Study the examples in this chapter and observe how some arrangements present a scalene triangle, evocative of the sky, mountains and ground. Others are static compositions that suggest dynamic movement, as seen in the photo on the left. Another technique of *ikebana* is to show the progression of life by combining the promise of unopened buds with fully open blossoms, as in the vase of lilies above. Freestyle arrangements have a place in *ikebana* as well, but only after basic techniques have been mastered. The so-called "thrown-in style" of *ikebana*, called *nagaire*, actually requires great care to achieve the desired angles.

Left The platform at the base of the *tokonoma* alcove is an appropriate place to display wisteria blossoms, in keeping with the spring season.
Opposite This arrangement is placed in front of a *tsuitate*, or free-standing screen. Notice how the glaze on the vase was allowed to drip a little before being fired, an intentional imperfection in keeping with *shibui*, the Japanese ideal of beauty.

Below left, center and right The space surrounding an *ikebana* arrangement is important, as it is intended to be viewed straight on. There is no limit to what can be used as a container, as long as it is capable of holding water.

FURNISHINGS AND ACCENTS

In creating a room that is true to Japanese aesthetics, it is helpful to blur the line between architecture and accessories. As cultural icon Sarah Susanka explains in her "Not-So-Big-House" philosophy, architects use the word "detail" to describe permanent features built right into the house itself, things that would not fall to the floor if one were "to turn the house upside down and shake it." However, as we have seen in the first two chapters of this book, *impermanence* is an intrinsic feature of Japanese design: interior walls may be removed to alter the size of a room; sliding *shoji* screens may be replaced by woven blinds for the summer; a room with no bed in sight may become sleeping quarters at night when *futon* are unfurled. In this chapter, we will show you a number of notable elements and discuss how they might be adapted to a Western interior.

As you will also see in the chapter, the line between form and function may also be indistinct. Closet doors may be painted with dramatic scenes evoking nature, or a prized storage chest might also be a staircase. Such versatility is liberating to the Western designer or home owner who may find ways of integrating Japanese furnishings and accents that have more to do with their beauty, or perhaps a new purpose, than with their original function. We may not wear *kimono*, but its unique shape

and exquisite patterns make it delightful as a wall hanging. The same is true for the painted folding screen, or *byobu*, which was originally used as a room partition or to block drafts of cold air. And even the most contemporary room outfitted with recessed lighting becomes more charming when bathed in the soft glow from a handmade Japanese lantern. The prominence of articles made from wood and paper in this chapter underscores their significance in Japanese design and speaks to the fine craftsmanship required to bring out their essence. The carpenter carefully selects and positions wood in his handiwork so that the grain may be appreciated. Wood with knots is not automatically shunned; rather, it is used intentionally for a particular effect. Indeed, it is often the juxtaposition of smooth, clean lines with the irregularities of materials as they are found in nature that yields the most dramatic result in Japanese homes.

Washi, literally Japanese paper, refers to paper that is made by hand. It figures in elements as diverse as sliding *shoji* screens that run the length of an entire building to oiled umbrellas that really do keep off the rain to the diminutive *origami* crane. As you will see here, the inter-play between paper and light is part of the appeal of *washi*, rewarding the perceptive observer with feelings of quiet and serenity.

A *kimono* with a design dyed over the entire surface is displayed as a work of art. The mountain range pattern on the *kimono*, blanketed with a profusion of blossoms and carp swimming up waterfalls, signifies early summer, as does the vase of blooming irises placed on a color-coordinated carpet to the left of the robe.

SHOJI SCREENS

It is an accepted fact that natural light has a positive effect on our psychological state of mind, enhancing creativity and productivity. It also helps reduce reliance on artificial light, thereby mitigating that increasingly familiar measure, the carbon footprint. This partly explains why *shoji* screens, sliding panels of paper attached to a wooden lattice, are perhaps the most popular Japanese design element incorporated into Western interiors. Versatile enough to complement almost any decorating style, and undeniably elegant, their fundamental role is twofold: to bring natural light into a room while diffusing the sun's glare, and to function as a window covering, room divider, or both. In today's home, they may also be used to conceal a closet or pantry.

Traditional *shoji* screens are made from handmade paper called *washi* that uses the bark of a few specific trees and shrubs, the most common being the bark of the paper mulberry tree. Replacement or repair of *shoji* was traditionally an annual chore, since the paper, while surprisingly strong, is susceptible to tearing. In between replacing the screens, repairing a hole or tear with a scrap of *shoji* paper was a common household task, providing an opportunity for artistic expression; a patch in the shape of a snowflake or cherry blossom casts distinctive shadows on the other side.

Today, innovations in the manufacture of *shoji* with more durable materials such as mylar or fiberglass abound, and we encourage you to explore the many attractive inserts that are available. In spite of the enhancements that improve the durability of the inserts, a skilled carpenter is still required to install a high quality *shoji* screen that glides smoothly along its tracks year after year.

Above Kickboards are both decorative and useful in a room where *shoji* are subject to heavy traffic. The use of a track along both the header and the floor is another important consideration in a busy room. Where the *shoji* are expected to remain stationary most of the time, installing an upper track may be adequate.

Above right *Shoji* panels used in place of drapes or blinds are compatible with Western-style furniture.

Right Light passes through *shoji* window coverings, highlighting the luxurious sheen of a lacquered box used to store a collection of decorative hairpins.

Left The design possibilities for *shoji* gridwork are infinite. The use of warp-resistant wood and a skilled carpenter are important to ensure the smooth operation of *shoji* for years to come.

Above Movable *shoji* screens
make an attractive "frame" for
the cherry trees in bloom in this
Tokyo garden.
Far left A ventilation window,
or *muso mado*, allows air to
circulate through its checkered
openings in this historic house.
Left Framed openings add a
sense of playfulness to the
design of these *shoji* screens.
Right Papier-mâché dolls made
in Fukushima Prefecture are
displayed against a backdrop
of *shoji* screens.

Left The indigo-dyed linen screens mounted in this room silhouette the garden, soften the bright light reflecting off the snow and protect the *tatami* mats from the sun's rays. In the process, the scene captures the essence of *shibui*, the Japanese ideal of understated beauty.

Right Each *sudare* blind in this Kyoto merchant's house has a tassel and hook that allow the blinds to be rolled up and out of the way, or unrolled to the floor as seen in this photo. *Sudare* that cover the entire opening are useful for keeping insects out while letting breezes in.

Below left to right In place of *shoji* screens (left), woven reed blinds have been hung from the tracks during summer. *Sudare* (center) have been unrolled all the way to a tiled courtyard. The narrow gaps between the reeds allow breezes to pass through and create rippling shadows on the modern courtyard floor. In place of a wide overhang or pergola (right), this contemporary home uses woven reed to extend the eaves during summer, when protection from the sun is needed most.

FABRIC AND BAMBOO B

Throughout Asia, matchstick blinds made from bamboo or reed a
and sun. Called *sudare* in Japan, they are hung from house eaves and u
when the main living room faces south, a practice that also maximizes
or tassels and hooks that enable them to be rolled up to the desired le
during summer, in winter the sun's glare from the snow may also be m
design work, we have used *sudare* to block the sun's glare but also to s

When a matchstick blind is mounted to a lightweight wooden frame, i
ing glass doors may be removed from their tracks and *yoshido* installed
provide subtle separation between rooms or between the interior and
at antique galleries and contemporary outlets that import items for the

DECORATIVE SCREENS
AND PARTITIONS

The Japanese painted screen, or *byobu*, is a masterpiece of form and
function. Part art, part architecture, the Japanese screen can function as
a movable wall, as a device to block unwanted views, or as a partition to
separate distinct activities within a large room, all the while serving as an
elegant work of art. Screens are mounted on lightweight hinged paper
frames, so in rooms with furniture they can be hung on the wall and
enjoyed as paintings without the inconvenience and extra expense of
wooden frames and heavy glass. Long sought after by collectors, antique
Japanese screens are now being discovered by interior designers for their
elegance and versatility.

A folding screen looks equally beautiful as a freestanding partition on the
floor or on a raised surface, such as a *tatami* platform. Freestanding folding
screens used as room partitions in Japanese homes come in sets of two
or six panels. A formal set consists of a pair of six-paneled screens containing
a scene that dramatically sweeps across the expanse of all twelve panels.

While folding screens can be hung flat across a wall like a conventional
piece of art, even more interesting is to mount the screen in such a way
that it preserves the folds for a more three-dimensional effect. Screens
are typically painted on gold- and silver-leafed paper, which produces a
lovely sheen and subtly reflects light. An aesthetically astute approach is to
co-ordinate the screen with the scenery outside the room, whether a pine
forest, a flock of birds or the waves of the ocean. Screens can be used to

Left Door latches on *fusuma* panels, known as *hikite*, are decorative items themselves.

Right These *fusuma*, which are being used as room dividers, have been painted with a scene of wild flowers bordering a stream.

Below The use of black ink, or *sumi,* on gold-leaf paper creates a forceful impression; this painting technique is known as *sumi-e*. The trunk of the pine tree, located right of center, is a fine example of the asymmetrical balance so important to Japanese aesthetics.

Below right The deep, mirror-like sheen of lacquer painted with flowers contrasts with these crisp white *fusuma* doors. As the flowers are considered sacred by some Buddhist sects, the doors are fitting for the altar room of this home on Japan's Noto Peninsula.

create stunning focal points in formal living rooms, while two-fold screens can create subtle backdrops for more intimate gatherings or can be placed on top of a *tansu* chest. It seems counter intuitive, but thoughtful placement of a Japanese screen actually opens up a room, even one of modest proportions.

Fusuma were traditionally used in Japan as sliding partitions to conceal closets or to divide interior rooms. Unlike sliding translucent *shoji* screens, *fusuma* are opaque and play no role in diffusing light. Rather, they were often used as a canvas for painting or covered with handmade paper, thereby contrasting pleasingly with the adjacent walls. Antique *fusuma* are difficult to find compared with *byobu*, but in some cases *fusuma* panels are refurbished and sold as *byobu*. Contemporary *fusuma*, which are available on both sides of the Pacific, are most likely to be partitions covered with textured paper.

Left Cheerful cherry blossoms, evocatively captured in so much of Japan's art and literature, wander across this span of panels that were once *fusuma* doors.

Above It is thought that one of the original functions of the *byobu* was to block drafts of cold air, hence the placement next to a *futon*. It is also particularly lovely when the folds are left intact, as seen in this depiction of chrysanthemums.

Right Before the advent and convenience of electricity, folding screen paintings on gold-leaf paper helped reflect light deep into a room's interior. The effect of this reflective surface, here a backdrop for a series of hawks perched atop a wooden gate, is still beautiful today.

Above left and right Painted morning glories and
cranes grace two sets of *fusuma* doors in this home
near Kyoto.

Left Painted fans adorn this two-paneled screen,
which makes an attractive backdrop for a table
setting.

Below A pair of *fusuma* doors depicts deer on a
silver background. Like gold-leaf paper, silver also
provides a beautiful surface on which light reflects.

Above These ornate *fusuma* doors are adorned,
atypically, with *shoji* insets. Such works of art often
evoke scenes of nature and the seasons.

Left Unusually, an antique Chinese *kang* table with a waist and cabriole legs is incorporated in this Japanese room. Low *kang* tables were traditionally used in China on a heated brick platform, or *kang*, for carrying out various household and leisure activities.

Right A variety of compartments and rich ironwork make this antique *tansu* useful in a hallway setting.

ANTIQUE **TABLES AND CHESTS**

Japanese tables, which range from all-purpose *kotatsu* to writing tables, were traditionally low to the floor and reflect both the fine carpentry of the Japanese as well as other traditional decorative techniques such as lacquer.

The Japanese love of wood and the need to store belongings gave rise to a range of chests collectively known as *tansu*. As the number of household possessions increased during the Meiji Restoration (1868–1912), carpenters set about constructing containers for virtually every possible item. Their beauty and usefulness has made them a major collector's item in the West.

Tansu range in style from plain to ornate, and various types of wood are used, so it is not difficult to find a shade of wood that is complementary to the Western furniture that you already own. Ironwork adorns many types of *tansu*, adding a dramatic accent to what is essentially a wooden box. A small chest might be used as a bedside table for a lamp and storage for reading material below while a large kitchen *tansu* is useful in a modern Western room, with compartments for items as diverse as fine china, CDs and board games. Small chests can be raised on iron stands to bring the proportions in line with the Western lifestyle and furniture.

The sliding compartments found in antique *tansu* are as easy to slide across their grooves as is a properly constructed *shoji* panel. The drawers, on the other hand, lack modern rollers, and while not difficult to use, they do not glide as well as the sliding compartments. The *getabako*, literally shoe box, is appropriate for entryways where Westerners are increasingly foregoing the wearing of shoes inside but lack an elegant storage solution, although the larger Western shoe might dictate the need for a custom-made piece.

Opposite A wheeled chest, or *kuruma dansu*, often held a family's most valuable possessions, since it could be pushed out the door in case of fire. Here, a handsome *kuruma dansu* stands proudly in a re-stored *minka* farmhouse near Kyoto.

Above The design of this piece evokes the staggered shelves so common to the decorative alcove, or *tokonoma*, of the tea room.

Left top and bottom Two variations of the step *tansu* chest, or *kaidan dansu*, illustrate how the space under the stairs was used efficiently for storage. The *tansu* itself is a staircase used to access the loft above or a second story.

FURNISHINGS AND ACCENTS

Above The board game *go*, played on a low wooden table, is popular throughout Asia.

Right *Isho dansu*, also known as *kimono dansu*, were originally used to store clothing but are useful beyond the bedroom. They are ideal for items related to living and dining areas, such as table linen, candles, even board games.

Above and below Lacquer sprinkled with powdered gold, a technique known as *maki-e*, was used to decorate this small writing table and *suzuri-bako*, a box used to store writing utensils. Many years of training are required to execute such intricate designs.

THE JAPANESE GARDEN

When Westerners are asked, "What comes to mind when you think of a Japanese garden?" a range of replies can be expected. Some people picture a large stroll garden with artificial hills and ponds, meandering paths and colorful *koi* swimming beneath a picturesque bridge. Dozens of such stroll gardens, known as *kaiyuu-shiki teien*, are open to the public in the West. The 2005 film *Memoirs of a Geisha* was filmed on location at several well-known gardens in California, including the San Francisco Japanese Tea Garden, Huntington Botanical Gardens and Hakone Gardens, reinforcing the romantic image of the stroll garden in its Western audience. Unless one's property is large, however, such a garden is difficult to create and maintain.

For the more modest sized back yard, there may be room for a *koi* pond or perhaps a cascading waterfall or stream. It may also be possible to incorporate artificial hills, known as *tsukiyama*, thus creating a garden with enough variety in the terrain for a stroll to become interesting, with surprises along the way. One must think carefully about how to hide and unfold the elements of a stroll garden so that not everything is revealed with the first step.

At the opposite end of the spectrum, rocks rule in the dry landscape garden, made most famous by Ryoan-ji, the Zen temple in Kyoto. Thanks in part to this ubiquitous image, an abstract scene composed of rocks and gravel and few, if any, plants is also topmost in the minds of many Westerners. Unlike the stroll garden, the dry landscape garden is intended to be viewed in its entirety from a fixed position as if it were an abstract painting.

To Westerners, the idea of a garden with few, if any, plants is no longer a peculiarity. Known as *karesansui*, literally dry–mountain–water, this type of garden is usually located within a limited space surrounded by walls and is characterized by an expanse of gravel with the strategic placement of stones. Its influence can be seen in many public spaces in the West, such as the rooftop garden at the School of Oriental and African Studies in London, the Noguchi Museum Sculptural Garden in New York City, and the entrance to the new city hall in San Jose, California, all of which invite the mind to contemplate the sculptural qualities of stone.

Between these two extremes are courtyard gardens (*tsuboniwa*), flat gardens (*hiraniwa*) and tea gardens (*chaniwa*). There is, however, an overlap among the styles that frees you to develop what works for you. Also remember that understatement is preferred over showiness. In this way, the plant lover must restrain himself and think about how plant material looks over the course of four seasons, and how the plants relate to each other. After all, the point of a Japanese garden is to relax rather than excite, to soothe rather than stimulate.

A lantern should be placed where it is assumed to be functional, such as alongside a path. This pedestal lantern also makes an attractive focal point at the end of this path.

FENCES AND GATES

For those who look upon a Japanese garden as a "scene" to be enjoyed from inside a house, the design of the outside boundary is important. Whether you enclose your garden with a plaster wall capped with a gabled roof of ceramic tiles or a wooden fence embellished with bamboo, it should be compatible with the architecture of the house while serving as a pleasing backdrop to your garden. It should also satisfy any questions of security and privacy you may have.

Fences that are lower in height and allow you to see through play a useful role in the garden. They can separate various spaces in the garden where visual continuity is still desired, such as between an outdoor dining space and a strolling area, or encourage visitors to look or move in a particular direction. We have also used Japanese-style fences to conceal pool equipment, garden hoses and garbage bins.

Beyond their functional role, some Japanese fences and gates also have a sense of discovery and playfulness, such as an unexpected window of lattice in an otherwise solid wall. Ornamental sleeve fences and wing fences placed perpendicular to the house extend the lines of the architecture while subtly differentiating spaces in the garden; the former is known in Japanese as *sodegaki* as its shape resembles that of a woman's *kimono* sleeve. The range of heights, shapes, and patterns used in bamboo fences alone is quite diverse, as you will see on these pages.

Above The entrance to a subtemple in Kyoto's Daitaokuji features a path bordered by a simple bamboo rail fence and walls topped with a tiled gabled roof.

Opposite The gate separating the outer garden from the inner garden in this Tokyo residence is made of bamboo and mounted on wooden posts. An outer and inner garden is customary in the layout of a tea garden, or *chaniwa*.

Left A wing fence, or *koetsugaki*, is usually placed at a right angle to a building. It may be purely decorative or it may gently divide or screen different areas of the garden.

Above A portable foot gate, placed along a path, indicates that the path is temporarily closed.

Above right, right and far right Black twine offers a visual contrast to the golden bamboo trunks used for the fences in these examples. The latticework in the wall in the photo far right allows a glimpse of the greenery beyond.

PATHWAYS
AND BRIDGES

Although the dry landscape garden is not designed to be entered since the patterns of carefully raked sand would be obliterated, most other types of Japanese gardens are intended for walking through. Indeed, a stroll garden uses paths skillfully to guide you through a game of "hide and reveal," where a series of vistas awaits you at every turn. Likewise, the primary role of the tea garden is to direct you along the *roji*, or "dewy path," in such a way that upon reaching the tea house your mind will be calm and focused on the tea ceremony.

Paved paths, or *nobedan*, are useful for linking the architecture with the garden. Create dynamic tension by combining cut stone pavers with more irregularly shaped stones. Random flagstone pieces with tightly fitted joints are preferred over obvious saw cuts as they are more in keeping with a naturalistic atmosphere. The same holds true for stepping stone paths, which are laid out in asymmetric fashion and weave through a bed of gravel or a soft carpet of moss.

For a garden with a pond or stream, large stepping stones called *suwatari* allow for a hopscotch type of crossing, while a bridge might bisect a large pond into two unequally sized bodies of water.

Opposite A stepping stone path disappears behind a low hedge of greenery, creating a sense of anticipation at what lies beyond. A large opening in the house frames the garden as if it were a painting.

Left The term *roji* refers to the "dewy path," sprinkled with water before the arrival of guests, that leads through the tea garden to the tea house.

Below A half-moon bridge invites exploration in this Osaka garden.

Top and above These pathways artistically combine stones of different sizes, shapes, textures and colors surrounded by gravel.

Right The best stepping stone paths include widely spaced stones of various shapes and sizes. The first stone should be large enough to function as a shoe stone, or *kutsunugi-ishi*, as shown here. Japanese sandals, or *geta*, have been placed on the shoe stone, thoughtfully pointing towards the garden so that they are easy to slip on.

Below A hedge and bamboo fence flank the sides of this informal path.
Bottom More formal than the stepping stone path, the *nobedan* assembles flagstone into a jigsaw of tight joints, enclosed by a cut stone border.

THE JAPANESE GARDEN

Above A staggered bridge of wooden planks
amidst a marsh of blooming irises is a beloved
image in Japanese poetry and literature.
Right This *nobedan* path juxtaposes closely
spaced natural stones, irregular in size and
shape, with larger cut rectangular stones.

Above A rustic stone path leads to a stone bridge and the temple beyond at Honen-in in Kyoto.

Below In the tea garden, a stepping stone path forces one to practice "mindfulness," to watch where one is going.

STONES, GRAVEL AND SAND

To think of a garden as a collection of plants is to miss an important element in Japanese gardens—stone. In contrast to plants that grow taller, change through the seasons and move in the wind, boulders, rocks and stones add mass and stability. It is useful here to return to the concept of *shibui*, or quiet, understated beauty, when considering how to select large boulders or smaller rocks and stones for a Japanese garden. Train your eye to look for rocks that reveal weathering and shaping over time. Specimens with lichens and moss are particularly prized for this reason.

Stone opens up versatile design possibilities. A rock can represent a mountain or an island, while gravel can suggest a creek or a sea. Combine boulders with cobbles and pebbles to form a dry streambed. The larger the rock material, the more forcefully the dry stream will appear to flow (see page 126).

Fine gravel—approximately one quarter to one half inch—is appropriate for raking into ripple-like patterns, as if the gravel were a body of water. Gravel of the consistency of fine sand can be raked into patterns as well, but limit its use to areas where wind and leaf debris will not be a problem, such as a covered courtyard.

Above and opposite Sand or gravel raked in patterns suggestive of flowing elements such as streams and clouds are integral to *karesansui*, or dry landscape gardens. In the photo on the opposite page, the *karensansui* style has been adapted to the courtyard garden, or *tsuboniwa*. Notice how the stones have been strategically placed at particular angles to suggest movement.

Left In the absence of actual water, rocks, large and small, form a dry streambed. **Below** Stones intended for foot traffic should be flat on top and spaced for comfortable walking. The weathered appearance of the stepping stones is in keeping with *shibui*, the Japanese ideal of beauty.

Above This flat garden, or *hiraniwa*, is intended to be viewed from a fixed position inside the house. Rather than fill up or crowd the space with plants, the fine gravel used here keeps the composition spare and serene.

Right A dry stream with well-placed boulders and stones can convey the same richness in topography as an actual stream.

Above Stone and gravel are the primary elements in the dry landscape garden, an abstract scene that uses little or no plant material. Exaggerated curves and mounds are characteristic of landscape architect Mirei Shigemori's twentieth-century interpretation of the *karesansui* style.
Right A stone wrapped in black twine signals that a particular path is closed. It may also simply be used as decoration.

WATER FEATURES

Water brings to the garden so many things—movement, sound, reflections, coolness—that it comes as no surprise that it is used extensively in Japanese gardens. A water feature may be as complex as a waterfall with multiple weirs or a pond stocked with iridescent *koi*, or as simple as a stone water basin or a reflecting pool.

Great skill is required to channel water to feed streams, ponds and waterfalls, while an even greater challenge is to make a waterfall or pond look natural, particularly in terms of having an irregular shape and different "arms," and in the placement of rocks. The examples on these pages demonstrate the feeling water brings to the garden, how it can be used in combination with the other basic structural elements in a Japanese garden—rocks and vegetation—and how it helps achieve a forest-like atmosphere and serene mood.

Manmade decorative water elements, particularly stone basins, provide subtle visual touches by reflecting the sky or nearby vegetation.

Left A small circle of water reflects the sky and the brilliant autumn foliage in this garden in the west of Japan.
Right *Koi* are prized in Japan and beyond for their colorful beauty. The overhang of this house extends over the water, making the water garden feel truly as if it is part of the living space.

Left and below The stone basin is a recognizable element of the Japanese tea garden. When water is routed through a bamboo pipe that recirculates, it brings the pleasing sound of water to the garden. Stone basins found in gardens other than tea gardens are often geometric in shape, as seen in the *chozubachi* to the left, carved in a block of granite at Ryoan-ji, Japan's most famous dry landscape garden. The arrangement of a low stone basin and surrounding rocks, seen in the photograph below, is known as a *tsukubai* ("crouching basin") and is usually found in tea gardens.

Right A stream flows through a lush moss garden at a Tokyo residence.

Right Jutting out over a pond and supported by posts sunk into large stones, this house is truly integrated with the garden. The close presence of water helps the interior feel cool on hot days.

Above Moss grows about the rim of this stone basin, or *chozubachi*, flanked by rocks of lesser height, at a house in Kyoto.
Above right A waterfall adds drama to a steeply sloping hillside.
Right Proper stone placement is important to achieve a natural-looking waterfall. A moss-topped stone lantern is included in the rock composition.

GARDEN DECORATIONS

A forest-like atmosphere, including the way stone and moss evoke the timeless forces of nature, is highly desirable in a Japanese garden. By contrast, decorative elements or artifacts add a human touch to a natural scene, reminding us that gardens are made by and for human beings. Some artifacts also have practical uses. Among the more common artifacts used to decorate the Japanese garden are lanterns and water basins.

The size and placement of a lantern is related to its aesthetic and practical function. A pedestal lantern (*tachi-doro*) or a buried lantern (*ikegomi-doro*) paired with a water basin placed close to the ground on a partially buried stone, is an arrangement common to the tea garden, where guests pause to rinse their hands and mouth before entering the tea house. Lanterns are also commonly placed alongside a path, where light might be needed. In contemporary gardens, it is suitable to place an accent light in the ground that shines upon the lantern, rather than to illuminate the light box within.

Opposite and left Basins of the "crouching" type (*tsukubai*), placed close to the ground on a partially buried stone, are most often located along the *roji*, the stepping stone path in the tea garden. The basin on the page opposite has been skillfully carved into the shape of a lotus. Water is introduced to the basin through a bamboo pipe. The *tsukubai* on the left is a natural stone with a bowl-like crevice carved out of the top. Elegant bamboo dippers laid across both basins are used for rinsing one's hands and mouth.

Far left Stone ornaments depicting animals or sacred figures are sometimes used as an accent in Japanese gardens. This one features a raccoon dog sitting atop a stone platform.

Left It is common to place a bamboo dipper across a *tsukubai*, or crouching-type stone basin, for rinsing one's hands or mouth.

Above A pedestal-style lantern, or *kasuga-toro*, stands a short distance from a *chozubachi*, a taller water basin carved from a geometric block of stone, traditionally placed next to a house.

Right An *oribe* buried shaft-type lantern, named for the famous sixteenth-century tea master, is the focal point of this Japanese garden.

Above Simple, humble materials such as bamboo poles fastened by cords add beauty to the garden when used for decorative effect.

Left A pedestal lantern and stone basin, unusually here with a lid, make a pleasing combination next to a moss-covered tree.

Above Bamboo sends up shoots in springtime, and the culms grow quickly to reach their mature height in just a few weeks. Spring is also the time to dig up young shoots that have not yet broken ground. These are a staple in traditional Japanese cuisine.

BIBLIOGRAPHY

Black, Alexandra and Murata, Noboru, *The Japanese House: Architecture and Interiors*, Boston, Vermont and Tokyo: Tuttle Publishing, 2000.

"Discover Shibui, the Word for the Highest Level in Beauty," *House Beautiful*, Vol. 102, No. 8, August 1960, New York.

Gong, Chadine Flood and Parramore, Lisa, *Living with Japanese Gardens*, Salt Lake City: Gibbs Smith, 2006.

"How to be Shibui with American Things," *House Beautiful*, Vol. 102, No. 9, September 1960, New York.

Itoh, Teiji and Futagawa, Yukio, *The Elegant Japanese House: Traditional Sukiya Architecture*, New York: Weatherhill, 1978.

Mehta, Geeta K. and Tada, Kimie, *Japan Style: Architecture, Interiors, Design*, Boston, Vermont and Tokyo: Tuttle Publishing, 2005.

_____, *Japanese Gardens: Tranquility, Simplicity, Harmony*, Vermont, Tokyo and Singapore: Tuttle Publishing, 2008.

Morse, Edward S., *Japanese Homes and Their Surroundings*, Boston, Vermont and Tokyo: Tuttle Publishing, 1989.

Rao, Peggy Landers and Mahoney, Jean, *Japanese Accents in Western Interiors*, Tokyo: Shufunotomo, 1988.

Saki, Akihiko and Brooke, Elizabeth Heilman, *Ryokan: Japan's Finest Spas and Inns*, Vermont: Tuttle Publishing, 2007.

Seike, Kiyoshi; Kudō, Masanobu; and Engel, David H., *A Japanese Touch for Your Garden*, Tokyo and New York: Kodansha International, 1980.

Seton, Allistair, *Collecting Japanese Antiques*, Boston, Vermont and Tokyo: Tuttle Publishing, 2004.

Susanka, Sarah, *Inside the Not-So-Big-House*, Newton, CT: The Taunton Press, 2005.

Ueda, Atsushi, *The Inner Harmony of the Japanese House*, Tokyo, New York, and London: Kodansha International, 1990.

Yagi, Koji, *A Japanese Touch for Your Home*, Tokyo and New York: Kodansha International, 1982.

Yanagi, Soetsu and Leach, Bernard, *The Unknown Craftsman: A Japanese Insight into Beauty*, New York, London and Tokyo: Kodansha, 1989.

ACKNOWLEDGMENTS

The authors are grateful for insights and explanations from Elaine Sakamoto regarding the art of *ikebana*, to John Larissou and Motomi Ui, experts on the Japanese tea ceremony. The authors would also like to thank the editorial staff at Tuttle Publishing as well as their enduringly supportive husbands, Svein Olslund and Dr Hayman Gong.

JAPANESE TERMS AND GLOSSARY

andon: a lamp made of paper stretched over a frame. It may be handheld or freestanding.

azumaya: an open-air thatched roof accessory building sometimes used in a tea garden as a place to sit and relax.

byobu: a painted folding screen traditionally placed on the floor as a room divider or for protection against drafts.

chawan: a cup or bowl without handles for preparing and drinking tea at a tea ceremony.

chigaidana: staggered shelves, usually placed adjacent to the decorative alcove in a tea room.

chaniwa: a tea garden.

chanoyu: the Japanese tea ceremony.

engawa: a veranda or corridor that runs parallel to a building, usually on the garden side of a house.

fusuma: opaque sliding partitions used for closet doors or as room dividers.

genkan: an entryway where shoes are removed prior to stepping up to the interior of a house.

getabako: a storage chest for shoes and sometimes umbrellas.

hibachi: a portable container filled with charcoal used to heat water for tea.

hikite: a finger pull, often decorative, used in sliding *fusuma* doors.

ikebana: Japanese flower arranging.

irori: an open hearth recessed into the floor of a traditional Japanese house.

jizaikagi: a hook suspended from the ceiling or rafters used to hold a pot or tea kettle.

karesansui: a dry landscape garden where rocks, water, or sand suggest the presence of water.

kotatsu: a low, wooden table with a built-in heater.

kutsunugi ishi: a shoe removal stone, placed in a *genkan* or next to the *engawa* where shoes are removed.

machiai: a covered waiting bench placed in a tea garden for guests to sit and rest before (or during intervals of) a tea ceremony.

machiya: a traditional wooden townhouse, usually with a narrow façade facing the street.

minka: a folk dwelling or farmhouse.

nijiriguchi: literally, crawling-in entrance, an opening to a tea room or tea house that requires one to bend or stoop, thus humbling oneself.

mizuya: an area or room adjacent to a tea room where tea wares are stored and preparations for the tea ceremony area are made.

ofuro: a Japanese soaking tub that one enters after washing to soak and relax.

roji: a stepping stone path in a tea garden, sometimes synonymous with the tea garden itself.

shibui: the highest level of beauty, characterized by simplicity, subtlety, and understated elegance.

shoji: translucent sliding partitions made of handmade *washi* or other translucent paper.

sudare: screens or blinds made of woven bamboo or reed.

sukiya-zukuri: an architectural style associated with the tea ceremony.

tansu: a wooden storage chest, of various sizes, often decorated with ironwork.

tatami: mats of woven straw, approximately 90 cm by 180 cm (3 feet by 6 feet), used as a unit of measurement for a Japanese room.

tokonoma: a recessed alcove in a Japanese tea room, used to display a scroll and flower arrangement.

washi: Japanese handmade paper, used for a wide variety of items, such as *shoji* screens, lamps and umbrellas.

yoshido: a screen or door made of reeds or bamboo that allows for ventilation.